BATHTUB TREATS

TABLE OF CONTENTS

INTRODUCTION

Thank you for the purchase of *Bathtub Treats: A Guide to Making Bath Bombs, Bath Truffles, and Bath Melts at Home Using All-Natural Skin-Nourishing Ingredients.* This book provides you with everything you need to know about creating your own nourishing and sweet-smelling bathtub treats to pamper your skin.

Nothing relaxes your body and mind like a hot bath after a long, stressful day. Baths help to relieve aching muscles as well as creating an overall calmness. However, hot baths can draw out the much-needed moisture from your skin, leaving your skin dry and patched. So, instead of adding toxic and expensive bath products that are usually packed with artificial colors and fragrances to your bath water, simply visit your pantry and make easy, quick bath products with natural ingredients.

Making your own natural bath products enables you to create non-toxic bathtub treats as well as customizing them with essential oils, dried flowers, and other organic additives. Thereby, helping you save more money compared to buying them from the stores. Most of the recipes contained in this book are anti-fungal and antibacterial, making them safe and perfect for use on every part of your body without clogging pores.

If you are the type that loves to unwind with a bath after a long day, you will certainly enjoy this book with the amazing bath bomb, bath truffle, and bath melt recipes it contains and you will also get inspired to develop your own recipes. You can make a big batch at once and give out to loved ones as gifts or store them for yourself to be used when you need some time to relieve stress, anxiety, or sore muscles as well as to enjoy some quiet relaxation.

Warm yourself up during the cold winter months with some homemade bathtub treats, slather on some detox face mask, light some candles, pour yourself some wine, blast some cool music and melt your stress and worries away in your own bathtub!!!

BATHTUB TREATS

There are many nourishing and skin-loving bath and body products you can easily make in your kitchen; bath bombs, bath truffles, and bath melts are terms you are probably familiar with. Although bath bombs are quite popular, bath truffles and bath melts are more recent discoveries. These bathtub treats help your skin to absorb some of the oils they contain when you soaking up, leaving your skin hydrated and smooth.

BATH BOMBS

Bath bombs are a hard-packed mixture of certain ingredients which fizzy when dropped into water. These bombs are used to add skin nourishing oils, butters, essential oils, color, bubbles, and scent to the bath. Bath bombs, also known as bath fizzies, are designed to take a relaxing bath to a completely new level. When a bath bomb hit your bath water, it'll start to fizz and bubble with aroma and colors. Some bath bombs have flower petals; some have sparkles while some simply make you smell and feel good. All bath bombs are made with natural moisturizers such as cocoa butter, shea butter, coconut oil etc. Most bath bombs contain restorative Epsom salt and therapeutic essential oils.

Making your own natural bath bombs enables you to create non-toxic bath bombs as well as customizing your bath fizz with essential oils, dried flowers, and other additives. Thereby, helping you save more money compared to buying the bath bombs from the stores. Whether you desire to have a revitalizing multilayered explosion of scent and color, petal-loaded floral soak, or just a relaxing bath, you can always make a bath bomb that's ideal for each bathing experience. Bath bombs need a dry climate and should be kept away from moisture to prevent fizzling before use. You can store bath bombs in a glass jar or plastic contain and place in your bathroom.

BATH TRUFFLES

Bath truffles are also a great way of adding skin-loving oils and additives to your bath and skin. Bath truffles contain more butter or oils than bath bombs, yet they produce lots of fizzes. Bubbling bath truffles add more fun to your bath as they give you luxurious bath experience and pamper your skin. You can also customize them with your desired carrier oils, butter, essential oils, colors, and scent. To use, break them up under a running faucet to activate creamy, fluffy bubbles.

However, be careful when getting out of your tub because bath truffles are packed with plenty oils and butter and will make your bathtub slippery. You can store bath truffles in a glass jar or plastic container and place in your bathroom. Bath truffles are a great gift idea for your friends and loved ones.

BATH MELTS

Bath melts releases skin-nourishing oils and butter into your bath water more subtly. The warmth of the water basically melts the butter and oils that made up the bath melts leaving your skin well hydrated and smooth. You can add herbs, scents, and colors to your bath melt as you desire. Bath melts do not fizz like bath bombs and bath truffles but they are easier and quicker to make. You can simply whip up some bath melts 30 minutes prior to your bath time. And you won't need to apply lotion or cream to your body after taking a bath with bath melts because your skin will be hydrated for about twenty-four hours, even in the dry winter period.

However, be very careful when getting out of your bathtub after having a bath with a bath melt because your tub will be slippery due to the large amounts of butter and oils bath melts contain. You can store your bath melts in the refrigerator to preserve the butter and oils and to keep them firm and nice if the weather becomes warmer.

NOURISHING ROSE MILK BATH BOMBS

This amazingly lovely bath bombs can be made with milk powder, rose petals and rose oil. The bath bombs will help to moisturize and nourish the skin. The rose essential oil helps to improve the scent of the rose petal while the milk powder makes the skin to feel and look smooth, soft and silky. This recipe will give you about 6 big balls and you may adjust it if you want.

Ingredients

- 8 oz. cornstarch

- 8 oz. citric acid

- 16 oz. baking soda

- 4 oz. dry milk

- 6 tbsp Epsom salt

- 30 drops Rose essential oil

- 6 tsp almond oil

- A handful of dried rose petals

- Food coloring

- Spritz water or witch hazel

- Molds of your choice

Directions

- Mix the dry ingredients in a large bowl.

- Add rose oil and almond oil and mix well to combine.

- Grab a handful of the mixture and squeeze to see if it

will hold its shape when you open your fist. If it doesn't hold together, that means it's too dry. Spray lightly with witch hazel or water to get a damp consistency. Don't overspray it or your mixture will lose its fizziness.

- Start filling your molds with the mixture. Press firmly into each half mold, and tightly close the mold.

- Allow the bath bombs to dry for 24 hours before you remove them from the molds.

- Drop a ball into a warm bath, hop in and enjoy.

- Place the rest of your bombs in an airtight container and store in a cool dry place.

EXOTIC TULIP-SHAPED BATH BOMBS

Create tulip flower shaped bombs with moisturizing coconut oil. You can try out a variety of colors and essential oils. This recipe will give you about 10 -12 bombs and you may adjust it if you want.

Ingredients

- 4 oz. cornstarch

- 4 oz. Epsom salt

- 8 oz. citric acid

- 16 oz. baking soda

- 30 drops lavender or your favorite essential oil

- 4 tbsp melted coconut oil

- 1 tsp cosmetic pigment powder

- Spritz water or witch hazel

- Tulip flower molds or molds of your choice

Directions

- Mix the dry ingredients in a large bowl. If you want to use multiple colors, separate the mixed dry ingredients into different bowls before adding cosmetic pigment powder.

- Mix melted coconut oil and essential oil in a small cup. Add to dry ingredients and mix well until combined.

- Grab a handful of the mixture and squeeze to see if it will hold its shape when you open your fist. If it doesn't hold together, that means it's too dry. Spray lightly with witch hazel or water to get a damp consistency. Don't overspray it or your mixture will lose its fizziness.

- Start filling your molds with the mixture. Press firmly into each mold.

- Allow the bath bombs to dry for 24 hours before you remove them from the molds. Flip the molds over and carefully press out your bath bombs.

- Drop one or two bombs into a warm bath, hop in and enjoy.

- Place the rest of your bombs in an airtight container and store in a cool dry place.

STIMULATING SEASIDE BATH BOMBS

This amazing recipe uses a combination of essential oils that make you feel like you are by the seaside and melt your stress away. Enjoy a completely relaxed bath in your tub with this recipe.

Ingredients

- 8 oz. citric acid

- 1 oz. cornstarch

- 16 oz. baking soda

- 4 teaspoons cream of tartar

- ½ teaspoon lake coloring

- 2 tablespoons apricot kernel oil

- 4 drops spearmint essential oil

- 8 drops lime essential oil

- 8 drops lavender essential oil

Directions

- Mix up baking soda, cornstarch, citric acid, cream of tartar, and coloring in a large bowl.

- Add essential oils and apricot kernel oil and mix well to combine.

- Grab a handful of the mixture and squeeze to see if it will hold its shape when you open your fist. If it doesn't hold together, that means it's too dry. Spray lightly with witch hazel or water to get a damp consistency. Don't overspray it or your mixture will

16

lose its fizziness.

- Start filling your molds with the mixture. Press firmly into each half mold, and tightly close the mold.

- Allow the bath bombs to dry for 24 hours before you remove them from the molds.

- Drop a ball into a warm bath, hop in and enjoy.

- Place the rest of your bombs in an airtight container and store in a cool dry place.

DELIGHTFUL CUPCAKE BATH BOMBS

The homemade cupcake bombs smell divine and look amazing. They will give you a sweet, floral, and citrus` scent that will enhance your bath. However, make sure you tell the kids that they're not real cupcakes and cannot be eaten. Cupcake bath bombs are very easy to make but you will make them in two steps; the first step for the base and the second step for yummy looking frosting. This recipe will give you about 10 bath bombs and you may adjust it if you want.

Ingredients

- 8 oz citric acid

- 8 oz. pink Himalayan salt/Epsom salt

- 16 oz. baking soda

- 4 – 8 tbsp melted coconut oil

- 20 drops orange essential oil

- 20 drops lavender essential oil

- Spritz water or witch hazel

- ½ tsp red food coloring

- 1½ cup powdered sugar

- 6 tbsp meringue powder

- Muffin cups or similar molds

Directions

Step 1:

- Mix citric acid, Himalayan/Epsom salt, and baking soda in a large bowl.

19

- Add melted coconut oil and essential oils. Mix until well combined.

- Grab a handful of the mixture and squeeze to see if it will hold its shape when you open your fist. If it doesn't hold together, that means it's too dry. Spray lightly with witch hazel or water to get a damp consistency. Don't overspray it or your mixture will lose its fizziness.

- Start filling your muffin tin/molds with the mixture. Press the mixture firmly into each mold.

- Turn the molds upside down and tap gently to release the bath bombs from the molds. Set aside.

Step 2:

- Stir the meringue powder into ½ cup of hot water and whisk with an electric whisk.

- Once the mixture becomes foamy and fluffy, add the powdered sugar slowly while stirring.

- Also add red food coloring.

- Next, pipe the pink frosting on top of the bath bombs with a piping bag. Begin the piping in the middle, and then go around the middle while you build up the frosting into a lovely peak.

- You may sprinkle some extra sparkles on your cupcakes if you like.

- Allow the cupcake bath bombs to dry for $3 - 4$ days before you start using.

SOOTHING BATH BOMBS FOR HEADACHE

This amazing bath bomb recipe is a great remedy for a headache. The bath bombs will also help you alleviate stress and relax you. This is a great gift idea for friends and family.

Ingredients

- 8 oz. cup cornstarch

- 8 oz. Epsom salt

- 8 oz. citric acid

- 16 oz. baking soda

- 1 oz. coconut oil

- 40 drops lavender & peppermint oils

- Food coloring

- Spritz water or witch hazel

- Molds of your choice

Directions

- Mix all dry ingredients in a big container.

- Add essential oils and coconut oil and mix well to combine.

- Grab a handful of the mixture and squeeze to see if it will hold its shape when you open your fist. If it doesn't hold together, that means it's too dry. Spray lightly with witch hazel or water to get a damp consistency. Don't overspray it or your mixture will

23

lose its fizziness.

- Start filling your molds with the mixture. Press firmly into each half mold, and tightly close the mold.

- Allow the bath bombs to dry for 24 hours before you remove them from the molds.

- Drop a ball into a warm bath, hop in and enjoy.

- Place the rest of your bombs in an airtight container and store in a cool dry place.

REJUVENATING MAUVE BATH BOMBS

This nourishing bomb can be made with mineral sea salt and lavender essential oil. It will help relax your muscle after a long, tired day as well as helping to rejuvenate your skin. This recipe will give you about 6 big balls and you may adjust it if you want.

Ingredients

- 16 oz. coarse mineral sea salt

- 8 oz. cornstarch

- 8 oz. citric acid

- 16 oz. baking soda

- 6 tbsp Epsom salt

- 6 tbsp melted coconut oil

- Isopropyl alcohol

- Purple mica powder

- 30 drops lavender essential oil

- Spritz water or witch hazel

- Glitter (optional)

- Molds of your choice

Directions

- Place a few drops of isopropyl alcohol in a small bowl. Add the mineral sea salts and two teaspoons of the mica powder and mix well to combine. You may add more alcohol or mica powder if required. Set aside.

- Mix the dry cornstarch, baking soda, citric acid and

Epsom salt in a large bowl.

- Add essential oil and melted coconut oil and mix well to combine.

- Grab a handful of the mixture and squeeze to see if it will hold its shape when you open your fist. If it doesn't hold together, that means it's too dry. Spray lightly with witch hazel or water to get a damp consistency. Don't overspray it or your mixture will lose its fizziness.

- Place some mineral salt mixture into one-half of the molds, and then fill up the remaining space and the other half mold with bath bomb mixture. Press firmly into each half mold, and tightly close the mold.

- Allow the bath bombs to dry for 24 hours before you

remove them from the molds.

- Remove the bombs from the molds carefully because a few of the salts may fall out when you open the mold.

- If you want, you may lightly dust glitter on top of the bombs to add shimmer.

- Drop a ball into a warm bath, hop in and enjoy.

- Place the rest of your bombs in an airtight container and store in a cool dry place.

KID-CALMING MICKEY BATH BOMBS

This delightful bath bombs idea can be a nice treat for your little ones. It will also help to calm and relax them. This recipe will give you about 12 bombs and you may adjust it if you want.

Ingredients

- 8 oz. cornstarch

- 8 oz. citric acid

- 16 oz. baking soda

- 6 tbsp Epsom salt

- 4 tsp almond oil

- 20 drops lavender or your favorite essential oil

- Spritz water or witch hazel

- Mickey candy decoration

- Mickey mold

Directions

- Mix the dry cornstarch, baking soda, citric acid and Epsom salt in a large bowl.

- Add essential oil and melted coconut oil and mix well to combine.

- Grab a handful of the mixture and squeeze to see if it will hold its shape when you open your fist. If it doesn't hold together, that means it's too dry. Spray lightly with witch hazel or water to get a damp consistency. Don't overspray it or your mixture will

lose its fizziness.

- Put a candy decoration in the center of the mold. Fill up the remaining space with bath bomb mixture. Press firmly into each mold and allow the bath bombs to dry for 24 hours before you remove them from the molds.

- Drop a bomb into a warm bath and let your kid soak for about 15 – 20 minutes.

- Place the rest of your bombs in an airtight container and store in a cool dry place.

EASY COCONUT OATMEAL BATH

BOMBS

Another amazing bathtub treats! When you're done bathing with these wonderful bath bombs, your skin will feel nourished and silkily smooth. You can make them with just five natural ingredients. Your little ones can also use them in bathing because they're so soothing and gentle. This recipe will give you about 6 to 8 big balls and you may adjust it if you want.

Ingredients

- 8 oz. sea salt

- 8 oz. citric acid

- 4 oz. oatmeal (crushed)

- 16 oz. baking soda

- 4 – 8 tbsp melted coconut oil

- Spritz water or witch hazel

- Molds of your choice

Directions

- Mix the dry ingredients in a large bowl.

- Add melted coconut oil and mix well to combine.

- Grab a handful of the mixture and squeeze to see if it will hold its shape when you open your fist. If it doesn't hold together, that means it's too dry. Spray lightly with witch hazel or water to get a damp consistency. Don't overspray it or your mixture will lose its fizziness.

- Start filling your molds with the mixture. Press firmly into each half mold, and tightly close the mold.

- Allow the bath bombs to dry for 24 hours before you remove them from the molds.

- Drop a ball into a warm bath, hop in and enjoy.

- Place the rest of your bombs in an airtight container and store in a cool dry place.

REFRESHING APRICOT BATH BOMBS

Making homemade bath bombs allows you to create natural, non-toxic bath bombs and you get to choose your own essential oil as well as extra embellishments such as dried flowers. This is a great recipe for everyone including your kids because of the non-toxic ingredients used. It also has a mild and relaxing scent. Enjoy.

Ingredients

- 8 oz. cornstarch

- 8 oz. citric acid

- 8 oz. Epsom salt

- 16 oz. baking soda

35

- 4 teaspoons apricot oil

- 30 drops grapefruit or lavender essential oil

- Spritz water or witch hazel

- Dried flowers

- Food coloring

- Non-toxic glitter

- Molds of your choice

Directions

- Mix the dry ingredients in a large bowl.

- Add apricot oil, essential oil, and food coloring, and mix well to combine.

- Grab a handful of the mixture and squeeze to see if it will hold its shape when you open your fist. If it doesn't hold together, that means it's too dry. Spray lightly with witch hazel or water to get a damp consistency. Don't overspray it or your mixture will lose its fizziness.

- Start filling your molds with the mixture. Press firmly into each half mold, and tightly close the mold.

- Allow the bath bombs to dry for 24 hours before you remove them from the molds.

- If you want, you may dust the bombs with glitter

- Drop a ball into a warm bath, hop in and enjoy.

- Place the rest of your bombs in an airtight container and store in a cool dry place.

FORTIFYING PUMPKIN SPICE BATH BOMBS

This amazing bath bomb recipe uses pumpkin spice, coffee butter, and powdered goat's milk. It absolutely nourishing and soothing to the skin and has a delicious aroma. This recipe will give you about 6 big balls and you may adjust it if you want.

Ingredients

- 8 oz. citric acid

- 8 oz. cornstarch

- 16 oz. baking soda

- 1 oz. melted coffee butter

- 2 tbsp goat milk (powdered)

- ½ tsp espresso fragrance oil

- ½ tbsp pumpkin spice fragrance oil

- Spritz water or witch hazel

- Orange mica

- Dutch cocoa powder (processed)

- Coffee beans (optional)

- Molds of your choice

Directions

- Mix the baking soda with cornstarch, citric acid, and powdered goat's milk in a large bowl.

- Mix up espresso and pumpkin spice fragrance oil and melted cocoa butter in a small bowl. Add the mixture to the dry ingredients and mix thoroughly until blended.

- Divide the mixture into three separate bowls while making one of them slightly larger.

- Leave the container with the larger bath bomb mixture uncolored.

- Add cocoa powder to the second bowl and mix well with a spoon or your hands.

- Add ¼ teaspoon of mica powder to the third bowl and mix thoroughly to combine.

- Grab a handful of the mixture and squeeze to see if it will hold its shape when you open your fist. If it doesn't hold together, that means it's too dry. Spray each bowl lightly with witch hazel or water while mixing to get a damp consistency (spritz the white mixture first, then the orange mixture, and the brown to avoid mixing the colors together). Don't overspray it or your mixture will lose its fizziness.

- Put some coffee beans in the middle of one of the molds and cover with some of the white bath bomb mixture. Press firmly into the mold. Then, place the brown mixture on the white and press down 'to condense.

- Fill the second half of the mold with the orange mixture until half full. Then, cover it with the white mixture and press down into the mold. Make sure each half of the mold is slightly overfilled with bath bomb mixture. Tightly close the mold.

- Allow the bath bombs to dry for 24 hours before you remove them from the molds.

- Drop a ball into a warm bath, hop in and enjoy.

- Place the rest of your bombs in an airtight container and store in a cool dry place.

NOTE: These bath bombs have 2 months shelf life due to the addition of powdered goat's milk.

ANXIETY RELIEF BATH BOMBS

This unique bath bomb recipe is filled with a wonderful aroma that will help to energize you and make your bath a delight. Make these lovely bath bombs at home to combat anxiety and stress and feel better and wonderful after using them in a warm bath.

Ingredients

- 8 oz. cornstarch

- 8 oz. Epsom salt

- 8 oz. citric acid

- 16 oz. baking soda

- 1 oz. almond oil

- 10 drops clary sage

- 10 drops chamomile

- 15 drops citrus/orange

- 15 drops grapefruit

- 10 drops lavender essential oil

- Mica powder (favorite color)

- Spritz water or witch hazel

- Molds of your choice

Directions

- Mix the dry ingredients in a large bowl.

- Add essential oils and almond oil and mix well to combine.

- Grab a handful of the mixture and squeeze to see if it

will hold its shape when you open your fist. If it doesn't hold together, that means it's too dry. Spray lightly with witch hazel or water to get a damp consistency. Don't overspray it or your mixture will lose its fizziness.

- Start filling your molds with the mixture. Press firmly into each half mold, and tightly close the mold.

- Allow the bath bombs to dry for 24 hours before you remove them from the molds.

- Drop a ball into a warm bath, hop in and enjoy.

- Place the rest of your bombs in an airtight container and store in a cool dry place.

RELAXING LOTUS FLOWER BATH BOMBS

This is an amazing bath bomb recipe that is so easy to make and it will help you relax as well as taking your mind off the gray skies and cold temperatures. Enjoy!

Ingredients

- 8 ounces cornstarch

- 8 ounces citric acid

- 16 ounces baking soda

- ½ tablespoon baby's breath fragrance oil

- 1 tablespoon lotus flower extract

- Jasmine flowers

- ⅛ teaspoon blue food coloring

- Spritz water or witch hazel

- Molds of your choice

Directions

- Combine baking soda, cornstarch, and citric acid in a large bowl.

- Add your blue mica to the mixture and mix well until well combined. If the color doesn't look deep enough, you can add more after you have mixed in the liquid ingredients.

- Add baby's breath fragrance oil and lotus flower extract, and mix well to combine.

- Grab a handful of the mixture and squeeze to see if it

will hold its shape when you open your fist. If it doesn't hold together, that means it's too dry. Spray lightly with witch hazel or water to get a damp consistency. Don't overspray it or your mixture will lose its fizziness.

- Put some jasmine flowers in the bath bomb mold. Place some bath bomb mixture on the flowers and press down (this is to prevent the flowers from shifting to the edges of the mold).

- Then, start filling the molds with the mixture. Press firmly into each half mold, and tightly close the mold.

- Allow the bath bombs to dry for 24 hours before you remove them from the molds.

- Drop a ball into a warm bath, hop in and enjoy.

- Place the rest of your bombs in an airtight container and store in a cool dry place.

HYDRATING COCOA BUTTER BATH BOMBS

These DIY bath bombs are great for a spa-like experience. Apart from the delicious cocoa butter aroma it gives you, it will also help to soothe and nourish your skin.

Ingredients

- 8 ounces cornstarch

- 8 ounces citric acid

- 16 ounces baking soda

- 4 tablespoons cocoa butter (for topping & mixture)

- ¼ teaspoon Dutch cocoa powder (processed)

50

- ½ tablespoon cocoa butter cashmere fragrance oil

- ½ tablespoon pure honey fragrance oil

- ½ tablespoon polysorbate 80

- coarse pink sea salt

- Spritz water or witch hazel

- Molds of your choice

Directions

- Mix baking soda, cornstarch, and citric acid in a large bowl.

- Melt two tablespoons of cocoa butter, your honey fragrance, and polysorbate 80 (helps to disperse the cocoa butter in the bathtub) to the dry ingredients and mix until well combined.

- Grab a handful of the mixture and squeeze to see if it

will hold its shape when you open your fist. If it doesn't hold together, that means it's too dry. Spray lightly with witch hazel or water to get a damp consistency. Don't overspray it or your mixture will lose its fizziness.

- Start filling your molds with the mixture. Press firmly into each half mold, and tightly close the mold.

- Allow the bath bombs to dry for 24 hours before you remove them from the molds.

- Slightly melt the remaining cocoa butter in the microwave and allow it to cool a little.

- Add cocoa butter fragrance oil and cocoa powder to the melted butter and mix.

- When the butter mixture thickens slightly, start

placing on the bath bombs. However, you need to work fast so that the butter mixture won't get too thick and if it does, warm up slightly for three to five seconds in the oven.

- Place a dollop of cocoa butter on each bomb with a spoon. Also, sprinkle pink sea salt on top of the butter on each bomb before the butter gets cool and hard.

- To use, drop a ball into a hot bath, hop in and enjoy.

- Place the rest of your bombs in an airtight container and store in a cool dry place.

Note: These bombs are quite fragile and may not be great for shipping. If you want to give them out as gifts, wrap them with care.

DETOXIFYING ROSE GOLD BATH BOMBS

These lovely bombs contain coconut oil, pink sea salt, and rose gold sparkle which gives the bath bombs a nice pop of color. These bath bombs also create a soothing experience for you in the tub.

Ingredients

- 8 ounces cornstarch

- 8 ounces citric acid

- 3 ounces coarse pink sea salt

- 8 ounces extra small pink sea salt

- 16 ounces baking soda

- 1 tablespoon rose quartz fragrance oil

- 6 tablespoons coconut oil

- ¼ teaspoon rose gold mica

- Spritz water or witch hazel

- Molds of your choice

Directions

- Combine the rose gold mica with the coarse pink sea salt in a small bowl.

- Place a small amount of the sea salt mixture at the bottom of the molds. Make sure you don't add too much to prevent the salt mixture from falling out when you remove the bath bombs from the molds.

- In another bowl, combine baking soda, corn starch,

citric acid, extra small pink sea salt, and the remaining coarse pink salt mixture. Mix until combined.

- Slightly melt your coconut oil and mix with rose quartz fragrance oil. Then, add to the dry ingredients and mix thoroughly.

- Grab a handful of the mixture and squeeze to see if it will hold its shape when you open your fist. If it doesn't hold together, that means it's too dry. Spray lightly with witch hazel or water to get a damp consistency. Don't overspray it or your mixture will lose its fizziness.

- Start filling your molds with the mixture. Press firmly into each half mold, and tightly close the mold.

- Allow the bath bombs to dry for 24 hours before you remove them from the molds.

- Drop a ball into a warm bath, hop in and enjoy.

- Place the rest of your bombs in an airtight container and store in a cool dry place.

REFRESHING RAINBOW BATH BOMBS

These bath bombs are amazing when they hit the water and begin to fizzy due to the rainbow that appears in your bath. They are soothing to the skin, smell wonderful and fun to make. They also make great gifts.

Ingredients

- 8 ounces citric acid

- 8 ounces cornstarch

- 8 ounces Epsom salt

- 16 ounces baking soda

- 20 drops essential oil (your favorite)

- cotton candy fragrance oil (optional)

- pink neon food coloring

- Rainbow nonpareils

- Silicone heart mold or molds of your choice

- Spritz water or witch hazel

Directions

- Mix baking soda, cornstarch, citric acid, and Epsom salt in a large bowl.

- Add food coloring, essential oil, and fragrance (optional) and mix well to combine.

- Grab a handful of the mixture and squeeze to see if it will hold its shape when you open your fist. If it doesn't hold together, that means it's too dry. Spray lightly with witch hazel or water to get a damp consistency. Don't overspray it or your mixture will lose its fizziness.

- Start filling your molds with the mixture. Press firmly into each half mold, and tightly close the mold.

- Sprinkle the rainbow nonpareils on top of your bombs. And you can also get the sprinkles on both sides of your bath bombs by shaking them into the molds before you fill the molds with bath bombs. If necessary, you can the back of a spoon to lightly press the sprinkles into your bath bombs.

- Allow the bath bombs to dry for 24 hours before you remove them from the molds.

- Drop one or two balls into a warm bath and watch the rainbow appear when they hit the water, hop in and enjoy.

- Place the rest of your bombs in an airtight container and store in a cool dry place.

MOISTURIZING HERBAL BATH BOMBS

These herbal bath bombs can be made with the moisturizing green tea extract. You will enjoy a relaxing and spa-like bath experience in your bathtub with this recipe.

Ingredients

- 8 ounces cornstarch

- 8 ounces citric acid

- 16 ounces baking soda

- ½ tablespoon Irish green food coloring

- ½ tablespoon green tea seed extract

- 2 tablespoons green tea seed oil

- Green tea leaves (optional)

- Spritz water or witch hazel

- Molds of your choice

Directions

- Mix up baking soda, cornstarch, and citric acid in a large bowl.

- Add green tea seed oil, green tea extract, and food coloring and mix well to combine.

- Grab a handful of the mixture and squeeze to see if it will hold its shape when you open your fist. If it doesn't hold together, that means it's too dry. Spray lightly with witch hazel or water to get a damp consistency. Don't overspray it or your mixture will lose its fizziness.

- Start filling your molds with the mixture. Press firmly into each half mold, and tightly close the mold.

- Allow the bath bombs to dry for 24 hours before you remove them from the molds.

- Drop a ball into a warm bath, hop in and enjoy.

- Place the rest of your bombs in an airtight container and store in a cool dry place.

GORGEOUS RASPBERRY JAM BATH TRUFFLES

This amazing bathtub treat uses raspberry jam fragrance oil which has a sweet aroma. This recipe will give you about 8 creamy and bubbly bath truffles. Enjoy!

Ingredients

- 16 ounces baking soda

- 8 ounces SLSA

- 5 ounces citric acid

- ½ cup shea butter

- ½ cup cocoa butter

- ¼ cup cream of tartar

- 1 tablespoon raspberry jam fragrance oil

- 1 ½ tablespoons polysorbate 80

- 2½ tablespoons liquid glycerin

- 1½ tablespoons raspberry seed oil

- 1/3 teaspoon poppy seeds

- 2/3 teaspoon raspberry mica

Directions

- Place raspberry seed oil, cocoa butter, and shea butter in a heat-safe bowl and melt in the microwave.

- Add liquid glycerin, Polysorbate 80, and raspberry jam fragrance oil to your melted butter and mix well to combine. Set the mixture aside.

- Combine cream of tartar, citric acid, and baking soda into a large bowl and mix well with a spoon. Add SLSA to the mixture and mix until combined (you may put on a mask to avoid breathing in SLSA since it is very fine and can easily become airborne).

- Put on gloves; add some of the oil mixture to the dry ingredients and mix with your hand. Continue to add the oils bit by bit to the dry ingredients and mix until well combined. The mixture should give you a texture that is soft, slightly sticky and workable (similar to bread dough). However, the texture of your mixture greatly depends on the melted butter temperature. The warmer the butter, the softer your dough will be.

- Divide the mixture into two bowls. Add raspberry mica into the first container and mix thoroughly.

Add poppy seeds to the second container and mix well.

- Place a sheet of wax paper on the counter and sprinkle some baking soda on it; this is to prevent the mixture from sticking to the sheet and to enable an easy rolling of the bath truffle.

- Place the pink bath truffle on the sheet and shape the mixture into a rectangular shape.

- Then, place the white bath truffle on the pink and spread it evenly until you create a flat rectangular shape.

- Using the wax paper, roll the bath truffle mixture and smooth out the roll if it sticks to the paper. Keep rolling until it forms a smooth, even log.

- When you have completely rolled the dough, use

your hand to shape it as you want; you can make it shorter or taller.

- Next, cut the log into bars with a sharp non-serrated knife. If your dough is very soft, it can be a bit sticky and will require gentle handling. So, cut the bars carefully or wait for about thirty minutes for it to harden a little.

- When you're done with cutting, place the bars on a piece of wax paper or parchment paper. You may give them a more uniform shape with your hands and smooth the edges. It takes about three to four hours for the truffles to harden.

- To use, drop a truffle into a warm bath or break it up under a running faucet to activate more bubble.

REGENERATING STRAWBERRY BATH

TRUFFLES

This bath truffle recipe uses geranium essential oil which is great for the body and mind as well as colloidal oatmeal which is a skin-loving additive. It is indeed a lovely recipe to try at home.

Ingredients

- 16 ounces baking soda

- 8 ounces SLSA

- 5 ounces citric acid

- ½ cup shea butter

- ½ cup cocoa butter

- ¼ cup cream of tartar

- 2 tablespoons Colloidal oatmeal

- 20 drops geranium essential oil

- 1 ½ tablespoons polysorbate 80

- 2½ tablespoons liquid glycerin

- 1½ teaspoons witch hazel

- Red food coloring

Directions

- Place cocoa butter and shea butter in a heat-safe bowl and melt in the microwave.

- Add liquid glycerin, polysorbate 80, and geranium essential oil to your melted butter and mix well to combine.

- Mix up the smallest dash of your red food coloring and witch hazel. Add the mixture to the butter mixture and mix until combined. Set the mixture aside.

- Combine cream of tartar, citric acid, baking soda, colloidal oatmeal into a large bowl and mix well with a spoon. Add SLSA to the mixture and mix until combined (you may put on a mask to avoid breathing in SLSA since it is very fine and can easily become airborne).

- Use a stand-up mixer to mix the ingredients or put on gloves and use your hands.

- Add some of the oil mixture to the dry ingredients and mix. Continue to add the oils bit by bit to the dry ingredients and mix until well combined. The mixture should give you a texture that is soft, slightly sticky and workable (similar to bread dough). However, the texture of your mixture greatly depends on the melted butter temperature. The warmer the butter, the softer your dough will be.

- Place a sheet of wax paper on the counter and scoop out bath truffles from your mixture with an ice cream scooper. It takes about three to four hours for the truffles to harden.

- To use, drop a truffle into a warm bath or break it up under a running faucet to activate more bubble.

MOISTURE-RICH CARAMEL BATH

TRUFFLE

These beautiful bath truffles are made with Epsom salt which is good for the skin, shea butter and cocoa butter which add lots of moisture to your bath, and polysorbate 80 which helps to disperse the butters in the bath. The bath truffles have a delicious aroma.

Ingredients

- 16 ounces baking soda

- 8 ounces SLSA

- 5 ounces citric acid

- 3 ounces cocoa butter

- 4 ounces shea butter

- 1.5 ounces cream of tartar

- ⅔ tablespoon burnt sugar fragrance oil

- ⅔ tablespoon polysorbate 80

- 2 tablespoons liquid glycerin

- Epsom salt, extra fine

- ½ teaspoon bronze mica

Directions

- Melt your cocoa butter and shea butter in the microwave using 30-60 bursts.

- Add liquid glycerin, polysorbate 80, and burnt sugar fragrance oil to the melted butter and mix well. Set aside.

- Mix up baking soda, cream of tartar, and citric acid. Then, add SLSA to the dry mixture (you may want to put on a mask when mixing in SLSA since it can become airborne easily and can be irritating if you breathe it in).

- When the butter mixture cools to about 180° F, add one-third of it to the dry ingredients. You need to put on gloves when mixing because butter mixture would be hot. And the hotter the butter mixture the softer your truffles will be. So, use your hands to mix the dry and liquid ingredients together.

- Continue to add the butter ingredients to the dry mixture bit by bit until well combined. The mixture should give you a texture that is soft, slightly sticky and workable (similar to bread dough).

- Divide the mixture into two bowls. Add the bronze

mica into one of the bowls and mix thoroughly.

- Place a sheet of wax paper on the counter and sprinkle some baking soda on it; this is to prevent the mixture from sticking to the sheet and to enable an easy rolling of the bath truffle.

- Place the brown bath truffle on the sheet and shape the mixture into a rectangular shape.

- Then, place the white bath truffle on the pink and spread it evenly until you create a flat rectangular shape.

- Using the wax paper, roll the bath truffle mixture and smooth out the roll if it sticks to the paper. Keep rolling until it forms a smooth, even log.

- When you have completely rolled the dough, use your hand to shape it as you want; you can make it shorter or taller. Then, sprinkle Epsom salt on top and gently press it into the log to help it stick.

- Next, cut the log into bars with a sharp non-serrated knife. If your dough is very soft, it can be a bit sticky and will require gentle handling. So, cut the bars carefully or wait for about thirty minutes for it to harden a little.

- When you're done with cutting, place the bars on a piece of wax paper or parchment paper. You may give them a more uniform shape with your hands and smooth the edges. You may sprinkle more Epsom salt on top if you want. It takes about three to four hours for the truffles to harden.

- To use, drop a truffle into a warm bath or break it up under a running faucet to activate more bubble.

NOURISHING GOAT'S MILK BATH TRUFFLE

The vanilla bath truffles give a wonderful and relaxing scent because they are fragranced with ylang-ylang essential oil. The goat's milk used for the recipe helps to soothe and soften your skin.

Ingredients

- 16 ounces baking soda

- 8 ounces SLSA

- 5 ounces citric acid

- ½ cup shea butter

79

- ½ cup cocoa butter

- ¼ cup cream of tartar

- 2 tablespoons goat's milk powder

- 20 drops ylang-ylang essential oil

- 1 ½ tablespoons polysorbate 80

- 2½ tablespoons liquid glycerin

Directions

- Place cocoa butter and shea butter in a heat-safe bowl and melt in the microwave.

- Add liquid glycerin, polysorbate 80, and ylang-ylang essential oil to your melted butter and mix well to combine. Set the mixture aside.

- Combine cream of tartar, citric acid, baking soda, goat's milk powder into a large bowl and mix well with a spoon. Add SLSA to the mixture and mix until combined (you may put on a mask to avoid breathing in SLSA since it is very fine and can easily become airborne).

- Use a stand-up mixer to mix the ingredients or put on gloves and use your hands.

- Add some of the oil mixture to the dry ingredients and mix. Continue to add the oils bit by bit to the dry ingredients and mix until well combined. The mixture should give you a texture that is soft, slightly sticky and workable (similar to bread dough). However, the texture of your mixture greatly depends on the melted butter temperature. The warmer the butter, the softer your dough will be.

- Place a sheet of wax paper on the counter and scoop out bath truffles from your mix with an ice cream scooper. It takes about three to four hours for the truffles to harden.

- To use, drop a truffle into a warm bath or break it up under a running faucet to activate more bubble.

RELAXING ROSE BATH TRUFFLES

These nourishing bath truffles are so easy to make. They look gorgeous and will leave your skin smooth and silky. You can customize the recipe with petals, colors, and essential oils as you desire.

Ingredients

- 16 ounces baking soda

- 8 ounces SLSA

- 5 ounces citric acid

- ½ cup shea butter

- ½ cup cocoa butter

- ¼ cup cream of tartar

- 1 ½ tablespoons polysorbate 80

- 2½ tablespoons liquid glycerin

- 20 drops Rose oil

- Rose petals

- Molds of your choice

Directions

- Melt your cocoa butter and shea butter in the microwave using 30-60 bursts.

- Add liquid glycerin, polysorbate 80, and Rose oil to the melted butter and mix well. Set aside.

- Mix up baking soda, cream of tartar, and citric acid. Then, add SLSA to the dry mixture (you may want to put on a mask when mixing in SLSA since it can become airborne easily and can be irritating if you breathe it in).

- When the butter mixture cools to about 180° F, add one-third of it to the dry ingredients. You need to put on gloves when mixing because butter mixture would be hot. And the hotter the butter mixture the softer your truffles will be. So, use your hands to mix the dry and liquid ingredients together.

- Continue to add the butter ingredients to the dry mixture bit by bit until well combined. The mixture should give you a texture that is soft, slightly sticky and workable (similar to bread dough).

- Place some rose petals in the bottom of your molds. Then, pack the bath truffle mixture into molds; cake cases, ice cube trays, or silicone molds.

- It takes about three to four hours for the truffles to harden.

- To use, drop a truffle into a warm bath or break it up under a running faucet to activate more bubble.

- Relax and enjoy your bubbling bath!

STIMULATING CHOCOLATE BATH TRUFFLE

These lovely bath treats are excellent gifts for your loved ones. The chocolate truffle has a sweet aroma due to the addition of midnight vanilla fragrance oil. This bath truffle recipe is soothing to the skin and will also help to relax your body and mind.

Ingredients

- 16 ounces baking soda

- 8 ounces SLSA

- 5 ounces citric acid

- ½ cup shea butter

- ½ cup cocoa butter

- ¼ cup cream of tartar

- 2 tablespoons cocoa powder

- 1 tablespoon midnight vanilla fragrance oil

- 1 ½ tablespoons polysorbate 80

- 2½ tablespoons liquid glycerin

Directions

- Place cocoa butter and shea butter in a heat-safe bowl and melt in the microwave.

- Add liquid glycerin, polysorbate 80, and midnight vanilla fragrance oil to your melted butter and mix well to combine. Set the mixture aside.

- Combine cream of tartar, citric acid, baking soda, cocoa powder into a large bowl and mix well with a spoon. Add SLSA to the mixture and mix until combined (you may put on a mask to avoid breathing in SLSA since it is very fine and can easily become airborne).

- Use a stand-up mixer to mix the ingredients or put on gloves and use your hands.

- Add some of the oil mixture to the dry ingredients and mix. Continue to add the oils bit by bit to the dry ingredients and mix until well combined. The mixture should give you a texture that is soft, slightly sticky and workable (similar to bread dough). However, the texture of your mixture greatly depends on the melted butter temperature. The warmer the butter, the softer your dough will be.

- Place a sheet of wax paper on the counter and scoop out bath truffles from your mix with an ice cream scooper. It takes about three to four hours for the truffles to harden.

- To use, drop a truffle into a warm bath or break it up under a running faucet to activate more bubble.

BEAUTIFUL MERMAID BATH

TRUFFLE

These gorgeous bath truffles are amazing. They create bubbles and fill up your tub with skin-loving oils. This recipe uses sea-inspired additives such as aqua pearl mica and course pink sea salt that makes you feel like you are at the beach whenever you are using them.

Ingredients

- 16 ounces baking soda

- 8 ounces SLSA

- 5 ounces citric acid

- ½ cup shea butter

- ½ cup cocoa butter

- ¼ cup cream of tartar

- 1 tablespoon island escape fragrance oil

- 1 ½ tablespoons polysorbate 80

- 2½ tablespoons liquid glycerin

- 1 teaspoon aqua pearly mica

- Coarse pink salt

- Gold mica (optional)

Directions

- Place cocoa butter and shea butter in a heat-safe bowl and melt in the microwave.

- Add liquid glycerin, polysorbate 80, and island escape fragrance oil to your melted butter and mix well to combine. Set the mixture aside.

- Combine cream of tartar, citric acid, and baking soda into a large bowl and mix well with a spoon. Add SLSA to the mixture and mix until combined (you may put on a mask to avoid breathing in SLSA since it is very fine and can easily become airborne).

- Put on gloves; add about ½ of the oil mixture to the dry ingredients and mix with your hand. Continue to add the oils bit by bit to the dry ingredients and mix until well combined. The mixture should give you a texture that is soft, slightly sticky and workable (similar to bread dough). However, the texture of your mixture greatly depends on the melted butter temperature. The warmer the butters, the softer your dough will be.

- Divide the mixture into two bowls. One bowl should

93

have about ⅔ of the dough while the other should have ⅓ of the mixture.

- Add the aqua pearl mica into the larger container and mix thoroughly.

- Place a sheet of wax paper on the counter and sprinkle some baking soda on it; this is to prevent the mixture from sticking to the sheet and to enable an easy rolling of the bath truffle.

- Place the blue bath truffle on the sheet and shape the mixture into a rectangular shape.

- Then, place the white bath truffle on the pink and spread it evenly until you create a flat rectangular shape.

- Using the wax paper, roll the bath truffle mixture and smooth out the roll if it sticks to the paper. Keep rolling until it forms a smooth, even log.

- When you have completely rolled the dough, use your hand to shape it as you want; you can make it shorter or taller. Then, sprinkle coarse pink sea salt on top of the dough and press the sea salt into the dough with your hand or a spoon.

- You may sprinkle some gold mica on the bath truffle if you want.

- Next, cut the log into bars with a sharp non-serrated knife. If your dough is very soft, it can be a bit sticky and will require gentle handling. So, cut the bars carefully or wait for about thirty minutes for it to harden a little.

- When you're done with cutting, place the bars on a piece of wax paper or parchment paper. You may give them a more uniform shape with your hands and smooth the edges. It takes about three to four hours for the truffles to harden.

- To use, drop a truffle into a warm bath or break it up under a running faucet to activate more bubble.

AROMATIC HERBAL BATH TRUFFLE

These nourishing and aromatic bath truffles contain herbs and essential oils that help you enjoy a spa-like bath in your own tub.

Ingredients

- 16 ounces baking soda

- 8 ounces SLSA

- 5 ounces citric acid

- ½ cup shea butter

- ½ cup cocoa butter

- ¼ cup cream of tartar

97

- 10 drops lemon essential oil

- 10 drops sweet orange essential oil

- 1 ½ tablespoons polysorbate 80

- 2½ tablespoons liquid glycerin

- 2 tbsp calendula blossoms, dried

- 2 tbsp lemon balm, dried

- 2 tbsp orange zest

- Molds of your choice

Directions

- Melt your cocoa butter and shea butter in the microwave using 30-60 bursts.

- Add liquid glycerin, polysorbate 80, and the essential oils to the melted butter and mix well. Set aside.

- Mix up baking soda, cream of tartar, citric acid, calendula blossoms, lemon balm, and orange zest. Then, add SLSA to the dry mixture (you may want to put on a mask when mixing in SLSA since it can become airborne easily and can be irritating if you breathe it in).

- When the butter mixture cools to about 180° F, add one-third of it to the dry ingredients. You need to put on gloves when mixing because butter mixture would be hot. And the hotter the butter mixture the softer your truffles will be. So, use your hands to mix the dry and liquid ingredients together.

- Continue to add the butter ingredients to the dry mixture bit by bit until well combined. The mixture should give you a texture that is soft, slightly sticky and workable (similar to bread dough).

- Pack the bath truffle mixture into molds; cake cases, ice cube trays, or silicone molds.

- It takes about three to four hours for the truffles to harden.

- To use, place a bath truffle in the bathtub for a slow fizzing reaction and little bubbles, but if you want more bubbles, break up the bath truffle under a running faucet.

- Relax and enjoy your bubbling bath!

CALMING LAVENDER BATH TRUFFLE

These luxuriously moisturizing bath truffles can be soothing and calming to your body. This recipe uses lavender petals and skin nourishing and softening butter. These bath truffles are even great for pregnant women due to the calming effect of lavender. However, consult your doctor before using if you're pregnant.

Ingredients

- 16 ounces baking soda

- 8 ounces SLSA

- 5 ounces citric acid

- ½ cup shea butter

- ½ cup cocoa butter

- ¼ cup cream of tartar

- 30 drops lavender essential oil

- 1 ½ tablespoons polysorbate 80

- 2½ tablespoons liquid glycerin

- Lavender petals

- Molds of your choice

Directions

- Melt your cocoa butter and shea butter in the microwave using 30-60 bursts.

- Add liquid glycerin, polysorbate 80, and lavender essential oil to the melted butter and mix well. Set aside.

- Mix up baking soda, cream of tartar, citric acid, and lavender petals. Then, add SLSA to the dry mixture (you may want to put on a mask when mixing in SLSA since it can become airborne easily and can be irritating if you breathe it in).

- When the butter mixture cools to about 180° F, add one-third of it to the dry ingredients. You need to put on gloves when mixing because butter mixture would be hot. And the hotter the butter mixture the softer your truffles will be. So, use your hands to mix the dry and liquid ingredients together.

- Continue to add the butter ingredients to the dry mixture bit by bit until well combined. The mixture should give you a texture that is soft, slightly sticky and workable (similar to bread dough).

- Pack the bath truffle mixture into molds; cake cases,

103

ice cube trays, or silicone molds.

- It takes about three to four hours for the truffles to harden.

- To use, place a bath truffle in the bathtub for a slow fizzing reaction and little bubbles, but if you want more bubbles, break up the bath truffle under a running faucet.

- Relax and enjoy your bubbling bath!

REFRESHING ORANGE BATH TRUFFLES

These beautiful bath truffles smell amazingly delicious due to the creamsicle fragrance oil used in the recipe. They are fun and easy to make and will leave your skin looking smooth and nourished.

Ingredients

- 16 ounces baking soda

- 8 ounces citric acid

- 3 tablespoons cocoa butter

- 5 tablespoons shea oil

- ⅓ tablespoon creamsicle fragrance oil

- Coral Orange Colorant

- 1½ tablespoons polysorbate 80

- Disk molds

Directions

- Melt your shea oil and cocoa butter in the microwave using 30 seconds bursts.

- Add creamsicle fragrance oil and polysorbate 80 to the melted butter and mix well. Set aside.

- Add baking soda and citric acid to a large bowl and mix.

- When the butter mixture cools to about 180° F, add one-third of it to the dry ingredients. You need to put on gloves when mixing because butter mixture would be hot. And the hotter the butter mixture the softer your truffles will be. So, use your hands to mix the dry and liquid ingredients together.

- Continue to add the butter ingredients to the dry mixture bit by bit until well combined.

- Divide the mixture into two bowls. Add drops of the orange colorant to one of the bowls and mix until well combined.

- Fill a mold half-way with the orange mixture, while pressing down into the mold, and then fill the rest of the mold with the white bath truffle and press down to fill up the mold.

- Place a cap on top of the mold and leave it for about three to four hours for the truffles to harden.

- To use, place a bath truffle in the bathtub and watch

it fizzy and fill your tub with nourishing butter and oil.

- Relax and enjoy your bubbling bath!

HYDRATING CITRUS COCONUT BATH MELT

These lovely bath melts are anti-fungal and antibacterial. They also have citrus and coconut aroma, including the fact that they are fun and easy to make. Using one of these bath melts in your bath will leave your skin hydrated for about 24 hours. You can also use the melts as an oil treatment for your hair since they're excellent for nourishing and moisturizing the scalp.

Ingredients

- 4 oz. virgin coconut oil

- Fresh citrus zests

109

- 10 drops orange or lemon essential oil

Directions

- Melt your coconut oil in a double boiler or microwave.

- Carefully remove from heat and stir in your citrus zests and essential oil.

- Spoon the mixture into ice cube tray or silicone ice cube mold.

- Set the tray in the refrigerator and allow them to harden for about 20 – 30 minutes.

- To use, drop one bath melt in a hot bath, hop in and enjoy your bath.

- Please, be careful when getting out of your bathtub because it will be slippery after using a melt in your

bath

You can also try these natural scents in your bath melts for more variety;

- Vanilla powder or vanilla extract

- Lavender essential oil or dried lavender buds

- Eucalyptus essential oil

THERAPEUTIC LAVENDER & HONEY

BATH MELT

This beautiful bath melt recipe is great for stress relief. The bath melts will help to relax your troubles and stress away after a long day, leaving your skin smooth and nourished.

Ingredients

- 16 oz. cocoa butter

- 16 oz. shea butter

- lavender essential oil

- ½ tsp dried lavender flowers

- ⅛ tsp honey lavender stress relief herbal tea (Yogi

brand)

- Silicone heart molds or your favorite

Directions

- Melt your butter in a microwave or double boiler.

- Remove from heat and stir in the herbal tea and lavender flowers.

- Pour the mixture into the molds and add two drops of essential oil into each mold.

- Place your bath melts in the refrigerator and allow them to harden for about 20 – 30 minutes.

- To use, drop one bath melt in a hot bath, hop in and enjoy your bath.

- Please, be careful when getting out of your bathtub because it will be slippery after yourbath.

SOOTHING ROSE & LAVENDER BATH MELT

These sweet-smelling bath melts are moisturizing to the skin, calming to the nerves, and soothing to the tired muscles. Use this recipe to enjoy relaxing baths whenever you desire.

Ingredients

- 1 oz. coconut oil

- 4 oz. unrefined organic shea butter

- 1 oz. baking soda

- ½ oz. red alaea salt

- ½ oz. dried lavender flowers

- ½ oz. dried rose buds

- 30 drops lavender essential oil

Directions

- Blend lavender flowers and rose petals in a blender until finely ground.

- Melt your shea butter in a double-boiler over low heat.

- Add coconut oil and the blended herbs, and stir for about to enable the herbs to release their healing oils.

- Remove from heat and allow cooling for about five minutes.

- Add essential oil, salt, and baking soda. Stir well to combine.

- Pour the bath melt mixture into silicone heart molds

or ice cube tray.

- Place in the refrigerator and allow hardening for about 20-30 minutes.

- To use, drop one bath melt in a hot bath, hop in and enjoy your bath.

- Please, be careful when getting out of your bathtub because it will be slippery after using a melt in your bath

RESTORATIVE PEPPERMINT BATH
MELT

Use this amazing bath melt recipe to pamper and nourish your skin and mind. The combination of lime, mint and healthy coconut oil in your bath melts gives a refreshing aroma as well as a lovely and healthy skin. Enjoy!

Ingredients

- 16 oz. coconut oil

- 1 organic lime zest

- Minced peppermint leaves (optional)

- 15 drops peppermint essential oils

- 15 drops lime essential oil

Directions

- Melt your coconut oil in a microwave or double boiler.

- Remove from heat and stir in essential oils when cooled.

- Sprinkle lime zest and minced peppermint leaves (if using) at the bottom of silicone molds.

- Pour the coconut oil and essential oil mixture into the molds on top of the zests.

- Place your bath melts in the refrigerator and allow them to harden for about 20 – 30 minutes.

- To use, drop one bath melt in a hot bath, hop in and enjoy your bath.

- Please, be careful when getting out of your bathtub because it will be slippery after using a melt in your bath.

EXFOLIATING HONEY MILK BATH MELT

These relaxing bath melts will totally moisturize dry, parched skin. They will also help to relax your body during bath time. This recipe contains honey which a great antibacterial and milk which helps to gently exfoliate the skin. The bath melts are excellent moisturizers for sensitive skin. Enjoy!

Ingredients

- 8 oz. powdered milk

- 2 oz. honey

- 2.5 oz. coconut oil

- 2.5 oz. Shea/Mango butter

- 4 oz. powdered milk (for rolling)

- 20 drops of essential oil

Directions

- Melt your honey, coconut oil, and mango/shea butter on a double boiler or microwave.

- Carefully remove from heat and stir in your powdered milk and essential oil.

- Spoon about 2 tablespoons of the mixture and roll into balls.

- Place the balls on a wax paper or parchment paper to cool.

- Then, roll the bath melts into the powdered milk (for rolling) to decorate them.

- To use, drop one bath melt in a hot bath, hop in and enjoy your bath.

- Please, be careful when getting out of your bathtub because it will be slippery after using a bath melt in your bath

REVITALIZING MATCHA TEA BATH MELT

These luxurious bath melts are great for a soothing winter soak, especially if your skin is dry and patched. This recipe contains matcha powder which has a high content of antioxidants, vitamins, and minerals which helps to exfoliate dry skin and repair damaged cell.

.

Ingredients

- 2 oz. shea butter

- 2 oz. cocoa butter

- ½ oz. matcha tea

- ½ oz. tablespoon honey

- ½ oz. beeswax

- 10 drops cedarwood or carrot essential oil

Directions

- Melt your coconut oil and shea butter in a double boiler or microwave.

- Carefully remove from heat and stir in your matcha tea, honey, and essential oil.

- Spoon the mixture into silicone molds or ice cube tray or silicone ice cube mold.

- Set the tray/molds in the refrigerator and allow them to harden for about 20 – 30 minutes.

- To use, drop one bath melt in a hot bath, hop in and enjoy your bath.

- Please, be careful when getting out of your bathtub

124

because it will be slippery after using a melt in your
bath

STRESS RELIEF OATMEAL BATH MELT

This is absolutely a great recipe to condition and pamper your skin. With the combination of honey, milk, and oatmeal, you will enjoy a soothing and relaxing bath that will help to ease your stress and worries. Enjoy!

Ingredients

- 2.5 oz. sea salt

- 4 oz. honey powder, milk, and oatmeal (blended)

- 4 oz. cocoa butter

- 20 drops Roman chamomile essential oil

126

- 3 tablespoons oat oil

- gold sparkle mica

Directions

- Melt your coconut butter in a microwave or double boiler.

- Carefully remove from heat and stir in your oat oil and essential oil.

- Sieve honey base, milk, and oatmeal and stir into the coconut oil.

- Mix up the gold mica and sea salt in a separate bowl.

- Sprinkle the mica mixture into your molds and top with bath melt mixture.

- Place in the refrigerator and allow them to harden for about 20 – 30 minutes.

127

- To use, drop one bath melt in a hot bath, hop in and enjoy your bath.

- Please, be careful when getting out of your bathtub because it will be slippery after using a melt in your bath

DETOXIFYING CALENDULA-INFUSED

BATH MELT

These beautiful bath melts have a fresh, clean, and spa-like aroma. The bath melts will also help you detoxify and relax your body. You can enjoy a spa-like bath in your own tub with this recipe.

Ingredients

- 1 teaspoon beeswax pastilles, white or yellow

- 4 oz. shea butter

- 4 oz. cocoa butter

- Dead sea salt

- Calendula flowers

- 30 drops of rice flower fragrance oil

- Silicone molds

Directions

- Melt your beeswax pastilles, cocoa butter and shea butter in a double boiler or microwave.

- Carefully remove from heat and stir in your rice flower fragrance oil when it is slightly cooled.

- For calendula infused bath melts, sprinkle calendula flowers in some of the molds' cavities and fill the rest of the molds with your bath melt mixture into silicone molds.

- For sea salt infused bath melts, spoon your bath melt mixture into your molds, and then add your sea salts on top of the bath melt mixture.

- Set the molds in the refrigerator and allow them to harden for about 20 – 30 minutes.

- To use, drop one bath melt in a hot bath, hop in and enjoy your bath.

- Please, be careful when getting out of your bathtub because it will be slippery after using a melt in your bath

-

EXOTIC ROSE & HONEY BATH MELTS

This is a luxurious, moisturizing bath melt recipe that is great for the skin. With these bath melts, you can enjoy a relaxing and soothing bath that will leave your skin nourished and healthy.

Ingredients

- ½ oz. oatmeal

- 6 oz. cocoa butter

- 1 oz. honey

- 10 drops ylang-ylang essential oil

- 10 drops geranium essential oil

- 10 drops rosewood essential oil

- rose petals

Directions

- Melt your cocoa butter in a double boiler or microwave.

- Carefully remove from heat and stir in your rose petals and essential oils when it cools.

- Spoon the mixture into silicone molds or ice cube tray or silicone ice cube mold.

- Set the tray/molds in the refrigerator and allow them to harden for about 20 – 30 minutes.

- To use, drop one bath melt in a hot bath, hop in and enjoy your bath.

- Please, be careful when getting out of your bathtub

because it will be slippery after using a melt in your

bath

ALSO BY LAURA K. COURTNEY

1. Bath Bombs

2. CBD-Rich Hemp Oil

3. All Natural Soap Making

4. Natural Healing with Essential Oils

5. Hair Care and Hair Growth Secrets

6. Clean Your Home with 66 Homemade Cleaning Products

7. Epsom Salt, Apple Cider Vinegar and Honey Natural Remedies

Made in the USA
Middletown, DE
08 December 2019